STUDY & MEDITATION

JAN
JOHNSON

6 STUDIES
FOR INDIVIDUALS
OR GROUPS

T0335280

Life
Builder
Study

INTER-VARSITY PRESS
36 Causton Street, London SW1P 4ST, England
Email: ivp@ivpbooks.com
Website: www.ivpbooks.com

Originally published in the United States of America in the LifeGuide® Bible Studies series in 2019 by InterVarsity Press, Downers Grove, Illinois
This edition published in Great Britain by Inter-Varsity Press 2019

British Library Cataloguing-in-Publication Data
A catalogue record for this book is available from the British Library.

ISBN: 978-1-78359-988-2
eBook ISBN: 978-1-78359-989-9

Printed in Great Britain by Ashford Colour Press Ltd, Gosport, Hampshire

Inter-Varsity Press publishes Christian books that are true to the Bible and that communicate the gospel, develop discipleship and strengthen the church for its mission in the world.

IVP originated within the Inter-Varsity Fellowship, now the Universities and Colleges Christian Fellowship, a student movement connecting Christian Unions in universities and colleges throughout Great Britain, and a member movement of the International Fellowship of Evangelical Students. Website: www.uccf.org.uk. That historic association is maintained, and all senior IVP staff and committee members subscribe to the UCCF Basis of Faith.

CONTENTS

GETTING THE
MOST OUT OF
STUDY & MEDITATION

H ave you ever wondered how God changes people? Maybe it seems as if old habits never change no matter how hard you try. Maybe you've become discouraged with your lack of growth into Christlikeness. You know that you are forgiven through Jesus' suffering on the cross, and you realize that you are totally accepted by God on that basis. This is wonderful. And yet your desire to live in a way that pleases God somehow constantly falls short of the mark.

God desires to transform our souls. This transformation occurs as we recognize that God created us to live in an interactive relationship with the Trinity. Our task is not to transform ourselves but to stay connected with God in as much of life as possible. As we pay attention to the nudges of the Holy Spirit, we become disciples of Christ. Our task is to do the connecting, while God does the perfecting.

As we connect with God, we gradually begin acting more like Christ. We become more likely to weep over our enemies instead of discrediting them. We're more likely to give up power instead of taking control. We're more likely to point out another's successes rather than grab the credit. Connecting with God changes us on the inside, and we slowly become the tenderhearted, conscientious people our families always wished we'd become. This transformation of our souls through the work of the Holy Spirit results in "Christ in you, the hope of glory" (Colossians 1:27).

God does in us what we cannot do by trying to be good. Trying to be good generally makes us obnoxious because it's so obvious that we're only trying. The goodness doesn't come from within ourselves. When we do succeed at being good, we subtly look down on those who don't do as well. Either way, we remain focused on self instead of on setting our hearts on things above.

Connecting with God, then, is important. But what does connecting with God look like? Through the work of the Holy Spirit, we copy Jesus in behind-the-scenes everyday activities he did to connect with God. As we let these activities become habits, we slowly become trained to have the heart of Christ and behave as he did. These activities are spiritual disciplines, also called spiritual exercises or strategies.

HOW SPIRITUAL DISCIPLINES WORK

We connect with God through spiritual disciplines or exercises. Study and meditation, the topics of these Bible studies, are two of them. Other disciplines include solitude, silence, worship, celebration, prayer, listening, service, secrecy, reflection, confession, fasting, simplicity, community, and submission. These exercises are studied in the other LifeBuilder Bible Studies. Still other disciplines can be used, some of which are written about in the classics of the faith and others God will show you. Henri Nouwen said that a spiritual discipline is anything that helps us practice "how to become attentive to that small voice and willing to respond when we hear it."*

How do spiritual disciplines help us connect with God?

- They build our relationship with God as we acquaint ourselves with the ways of God. (It's possible, of course, to do these disciplines in a legalistic way and never bond with Christ.)
- They build our trust in Christ. Some of the disciplines are uncomfortable. You have to go out on a limb. You try fasting, and you don't die. You serve someone, and it turns out to be fun and enriching.
- They force us to make little decisions that multiply. Your little decision to abstain from watching a television show helps you to deny yourself and love others in all sorts of ways.
- They reorganize our impulses so that obedience is more natural.

For example, if you have a spiritual discipline of practicing the presence of God, you may learn to automatically pray the breath prayer "Into Thy Hands" when someone opposes you. Without your realizing it, your opponent is no longer an adversary but a person God is dealing with or perhaps even speaking through in some way.

- They help us eventually behave like Christ—but this is by God's miraculous work, not our direct effort.

- They teach us to trust that God will do the work in our inner being through the power of the Spirit (Ephesians 3:16). Your spirituality is not about you; it's the work of God in you. You get to cooperate in God's "family business" of transforming the world.

HOW WE GET SPIRITUAL DISCIPLINES WRONG

Spiritual exercises must be done with the goal of connecting, not for any sake of their own or any desire to check them off a list of to-do items. If you read your Bible just to get it done or because you've heard this will help you have a better day, you'll be anxious to complete the Bible study questions or to get to the bottom of the page of today's reading. But if your goal in Bible reading is to connect with God, you may pause whenever you sense God speaking to you. You'll stop and meditate on it. You may pray certain phrases back to God, indicating your needs or your wishes or your questions. You may choose to read that passage day after day for a month because God keeps using it to speak to you.

After such a session, you will have a stronger desire to connect with God. That little choice you made to connect will leave you slightly different for life.

The exercise or discipline is beneficial because it helps you practice connecting with God. If you want to play the piano well or swing a tennis racket well, you have to practice certain exercises over and over. Good baseball players train behind-the-scenes by practicing their batting day after day, with no crowds watching. That's what spiritual disciplines or exercises are about. If you can hear God in Bible study and meditation, you'll more likely hear God in a board meeting or an altercation with a recalcitrant teen when passions run high. In life with God, we get good at connecting on an everyday basis by devoting time to developing the skills needed.

THE DISCIPLINES OF BIBLE STUDY AND MEDITATION

The techniques of Bible study are familiar to many—observing the facts of Scripture, interpreting it in light of its historical and biblical context, and thinking of ways to put it into practice. Meditation on Scripture, however, is very different. Here's a comparison.

In the study method, you . . .	In the meditation method, you . . .
dissect the text	savor the text and enter into it
ask questions about the text	let the text ask questions of you
read and compare facts and new ways	read to let God speak to you (in light of facts already established)**
apply facts	

The Bible doesn't instruct us on how to meditate for the same reason it doesn't instruct us on how to fast. These were common spiritual disciplines of the day that folks already knew how to do, or they knew other folks who did. Through the ages, the mechanics of meditation have been kept alive mostly through monastic communities. The two most common methods of meditation are presented in sessions five and six.

Bible study is an excellent way of setting oneself up for meditation because through it you come to understand the main point of the Scripture. Still, study does not rule meditation. God may help you choose an obscure word in the passage to ponder or point out a sideline character for you to identify with. Each time you meditate on the passage, it's likely to be different because you will be in a different set of circumstances.

USING THESE STUDIES IN RETREATS

These studies work well for an individual taking a personal retreat. Simply do the studies at your own pace, and do not rush them. Allow enough time to do the transformation exercises as well. Don't feel you have to do all the studies. In fact, you may wish to focus only on one discipline and use only those studies.

A group wishing to explore certain disciplines can also use one of these studies the same way. Be sure to allow time for participants to do the transformation exercises. Some exercises may be done as a group. Others may be done individually, with group members reporting back to each other about how they heard God during the exercise.

For either type of retreat, allow plenty of time for pondering. May these studies help you move a few steps closer to living your life in union with God.

SUGGESTIONS FOR INDIVIDUAL STUDY

1. As you begin each study, pray that God will speak to you through his Word.

2. Read the introduction to the study and respond to the personal reflection question or exercise. This is designed to help you focus on God and on the theme of the study.

3. Each study deals with a particular passage so that you can delve into the author's meaning in that context. Read and re-read the passage to be studied. The questions are written using the language of the New International Version, so you may wish to use that version of the Bible. The New Revised Standard Version is also recommended.

4. This is an inductive Bible study, designed to help you discover for yourself what Scripture is saying. The study includes three types of questions. Observation questions ask about the basic facts: who, what, when, where, and how. Interpretation questions delve into the meaning of the passage. Application questions help you discover the implications of the text for growing in Christ. These three keys unlock the treasures of Scripture.

Write your answers to the questions in the spaces provided or in a personal journal. Writing can bring clarity and deeper understanding of yourself and of God's Word.

5. It might be good to have a Bible dictionary handy. Use it to look up any unfamiliar words, names, or places.

6. Use the prayer suggestion to guide you in thanking God for what you have learned and to pray about the applications that have come to mind.

7. You may want to go on to the suggestion under "Now or Later," or you may want to use that idea for your next study.

SUGGESTIONS FOR MEMBERS OF A GROUP STUDY

1. Come to the study prepared. Follow the suggestions for individual study mentioned above. You will find that careful preparation will greatly enrich your time spent in group discussion.

2. Be willing to participate in the discussion. The leader of your group will not be lecturing. Instead, he or she will be encouraging the members of the group to discuss what they have learned. The leader will be asking the questions that are found in this guide.

3. Stick to the topic being discussed. Your answers should be based on the verses that are the focus of the discussion and not on outside authorities such as commentaries or speakers. These studies focus on a particular passage of Scripture. Only rarely should you refer to other portions of the Bible. This allows for everyone to participate in in-depth study on equal ground.

4. Be sensitive to the other members of the group. Listen attentively when they describe what they have learned. You may be surprised by their insights! Each question assumes a variety of answers. Many questions do not have "right" answers, particularly questions that aim at meaning or application. Instead the questions push us to explore the passage more thoroughly.

When possible, link what you say to the comments of others. Also, be affirming whenever you can. This will encourage some of the more hesitant members of the group to participate.

5. Be careful not to dominate the discussion. We are sometimes so eager to express our thoughts that we leave too little opportunity for others to respond. By all means participate! But allow others to also.

6. Expect God to teach you through the passage being discussed and through the other members of the group. Pray that you will have an enjoyable and profitable time together, but also that as a result of the study you will find ways that you can take action individually or as a group.

7. Remember that anything said in the group is considered confidential and should not be discussed outside the group unless specific permission is given to do so.

8. If you are the group leader, you will find additional suggestions at the back of the guide.

---

*Henri Nouwen, *Making All Things New* (San Francisco: HarperSanFrancisco, 1981), 66.
**This comparison originated from and is expanded in Dallas Willard, *The Spirit of the Disciplines* (San Francisco: Harper & Row, 1988), 3.

ONE

IMMERSING YOURSELF IN GOD'S THOUGHTS

Deuteronomy 6:1-9

D ead words on a page. That's how folks often approach Bible reading and study. So they long for an exciting teacher to make the words come alive.

Yet the words of Scripture are God-breathed (2 Timothy 3:16). God uses them to connect with us and communicate to us what genuine goodness is. Inhaling these carefully breathed words of life can transform us into radically different people who think as God thinks and love as God loves.

Bible study, then, involves more than examination of facts. It's a communication of who God is and an immersion into God's counsel for living wisely. Each day as we read God's Word, God imparts to us a little more of what we need to know. We can look forward to hearing from God every day as we read Scripture.

Group Discussion. What moves a person from reading the Bible only out of obligation to desiring to read it and connect with God?

Personal Reflection. When is the last time you found yourself reveling in Scripture and its message?

In today's passage, Moses reviews God's directives for the nation of Israel so they can live a life of wholeness and goodness as they enter the Promised Land. *Read Deuteronomy 6:1-9.*

1. If the Israelites observed the commands of Scripture, what two results would follow?

2. How do these results challenge the common idea that doing what God commands will ruin your life and make it boring?

3. What does the text say would be the results of being "careful to obey" God?

4. How do these first three verses support the idea that God is *for* us, wanting to produce in us a life that is whole and good in the deepest sense?

5. What do the statements in these verses reveal about how we relate to God (especially compared to cultural ideas of legalism and obligation)?

6. Why would love for God and trust in God's motives make us more eager to learn what God thinks about our human life and the way it works ("these commandments")?

7. How might day-to-day conversations about God and what God wants for us (decrees, laws, and commands) help parents connect with God as well as their children (vv. 7-9)?

8. What do these verses tell us about letting our life with God permeate all of our ordinary, mundane activities?

9. How do the truths in verses 1-9 help us know that God is looking for more than a righteousness based only on outward behaviors?

10. Second Timothy 3:16 talks about Scripture as being "God-breathed." How would you describe what God is breathing into us through our reading of Scripture?

11. How do you think people who have thoroughly immersed themselves in the wisdom of the Scriptures are likely to be different from other folks?

12. Sit in quiet for at least ten minutes and list situations and locations in your life (committee meeting rooms, relationship with a family member) where your attitude could be transformed by saying aloud or praying to God silently a passage such as one of these:

> As the deer pants for streams of water,
> so my soul pants for you, my God.
> My soul thirsts for God, for the living God.
> When can I go and meet with God? . . .
> Why, my soul, are you downcast?
> Why so disturbed within me?
> Put your hope in God,
> for I will yet praise him,
> my Savior and my God. (Psalm 42:1-2, 5)

What word or phrase stood out to you in this passage?

 Ask God to use these studies to bring Scripture alive to you.

████████████████████ NOW OR LATER ████████████████████

Experiment with one or more of the following.

- Pretend to be a poet. List some nurturing and plentiful images for times of reading Scripture to finish this sentence: *Reading Scripture fills me with God the way . . .*

- □ a clear, majestic day of fishing (or surfing) does
- □ a lean, flavorful gourmet meal does
- □ a baby needing to be rocked and finding contentment in your arms does
- □ a late-night, close-to-the-bone conversation does
- □ the disciples burned with truth and wisdom on the road to Emmaus as Jesus explained things
- □ something else?

- Journal about how much you do and don't trust God to do good things in your life. Or make a photo album or video diary showing areas in your life where you trust God and areas where you need to trust him more. Don't be afraid to admit it if you don't trust God that way but would like to.

- Write Psalm 42:1-2, 5 on a small card and memorize it as you jog or walk, letting the psalmist's words linger in your mind as you reflect on them. Careful crossing the roads!

TWO

READING AND RESPONDING TO SCRIPTURE

Nehemiah 8:1-18; 9:1-3, 38

*C*ompartmentalized. That word describes how we often approach God's Word. We read it (physical act only); we study and interpret it (intellectual only); we sing it (worship only); we apply it (facing our will only). But the elements of processing Scripture—reading it, studying it, meditating on it, waiting on it, worshiping God, delighting in God, praying it back to God—are all of a piece. For the Israelites the reading of the Law was not a one-mode activity. They put all of themselves into it, and they responded with all of themselves. They absorbed it.

Group Discussion. Picture yourself having just read some verses of Scripture. Which of the following thoughts characterize your most common response to it? (Circle two or three, if you wish.)

- What in the world did that mean?
- I wish I were as smart as so-and-so; then I could understand this.
- I remember a sermon about this passage—now, what did it say this meant?
- I could never do what this passage commands.
- I wish I could be like that person (or ideal) described in the passage.
- That was new!
- I already knew that!
- That's done. Now it's time to take care of the next thing on my to-do list.
- I'm so sleepy . . .
- Something else?

Personal Reflection. Recall your earliest experiences with Scripture. When has it been powerful for you?

Today's passage describes a worship service at a peak moment in Israel's history. The remnant of Judah that returned from Persia not only survived but also rebuilt Jerusalem's walls. They worked hard and trusted God well. And God gave them what they had longed for—they were once again safe in their homeland. Now it was time to continue their conversation with God, and so they listened to the Word. Let's look at how they processed Scripture. They set an example for us of letting God-breathed words interrupt their lives, with the expectation that God would speak to them. They heard and responded in a variety of ways. *Read Nehemiah 8:1-9.*

1. Why are the activities described in verse 1 an appropriate response after God had enabled the Israelites to rebuild the walls of Jerusalem in just fifty-two days (Nehemiah 1-7)?

2. Describe the listeners and how they listened.

3. How did the people respond to Ezra opening the Book of the Law?

4. What does the example of Ezra and the Levites "making [the Law] clear" tell us about what we may need to do when reading Scripture?

5. As the instruction continued, how did the people respond (v. 9)?

6. What do these responses indicate about the importance of expecting to hear from God and responding in some way when Scripture is read?

7. *Read Nehemiah 8:10-18.* What did Nehemiah and the Levites urge the people to do instead of to weep (vv. 10-12)? Why was this a good idea?

8. What else did the people do in response to hearing Scripture (vv. 14-17)?

9. *Read Nehemiah 9:1-3, 38.* In what other ways did the people respond to hearing Scripture?

10. Which of the following responses to Scripture would you like to try more often? Why?

- praying
- worshiping
- weeping
- celebrating
- confessing sin

11. Why is a person who connects with God through Scripture as the Israelites did likely to be changed?

12. What gesture of response from this passage (such as lifting hands or bowing with your face to the ground [v. 6]) would you like to incorporate into your own prayer life?

If you are comfortable, as you finish this study, pray to God using a physical gesture of prayer.

NOW OR LATER

Experiment with one or more of the following.

- Read Ephesians 1:1-12 aloud slowly. Which word or phrase is most meaningful to you? Why? What does that phrase tell you about how you want to connect with God? If you were to pray phrases from Ephesians 1:1-12 back to God, what would you pray? Here are some starters:

  ☐ Open my eyes, O God, to the rich things you're blessing me with that I don't see or understand (v. 3).

  ☐ Thank you, O God, that you loved the idea of me before I was born—even though I tend to think the idea of me is inadequate (vv. 4-5).

- Journal about the "joy of the Lord" and its relationship to Scripture. Here's an idea to get you started: The joy of the Lord is a "joy founded on the feeling of the communion with the Lord, on the consciousness that we have in the Lord a God long-suffering and abundant in goodness and truth."

- Give yourself permission to have a good cry about your relationship with God: how much God loves you; how you may have ignored God; how much God has helped you. Or, in lieu of a cry, go for a walk or run and talk aloud to God.

---

*C. F. Keil, Commentary on the Old Testament, vol. 3, I and II Kings, I and II Chronicles, Ezra, Nehemiah, Esther (Grand Rapids: Eerdmans, 1973), 232.

THREE

COMPREHENDING GOD'S TRUTH

Isaiah 11:1-9

I don't get it" is the phrase we use to indicate that we don't comprehend the meaning of what we read or heard. The purpose of studying the Bible is to "get it." We examine the text carefully to comprehend what the Holy Spirit is communicating through the words on the page. Although the Scripture itself says almost nothing about study, it does urge us to make the effort required to truly hear the Word and follow it, both of which involve comprehension. The goal of studying Scripture is to know God.

Genuine study occurs in many ways. One common method is to ask questions about the text such as these.

1. *Gathering basic facts.* What does this passage say? Who is speaking and who is being spoken to? Based on the historical background, what did the author intend for it to say?

2. *Understanding the text.* What does this passage say about what God is like? What does it say about human nature? What does it say about how God relates to people?

3. *Applying the text.* What does the passage suggest about how I might pray? What does it suggest about how I might act?

The first kind of questions helps us collect facts in order to answer the second kind, which works toward comprehension (or understanding). We connect the dots between this new information and what we already know. Sometimes the new information makes ideas more clear; other times, it contradicts what we already know and challenges us to think more deeply. The third kind of questions helps us reflect on the significance of the passage and ask God to show us how we might put it into practice.

Group Discussion. What has helped you the most in understanding the Bible?

Personal Reflection. Which of the three kinds of questions is easiest for you? Which is most difficult for you?

The questions below follow the flow of the three kinds of questions mentioned above. The background for this passage is that Isaiah is speaking to the southern kingdom of Judah, who keeps turning its back on God and is soon to be taken into captivity. Besides warning Judah of this, Isaiah also offers hope about the "shoot" or "Branch" (the Messiah, or Davidic King, who is Jesus) that would come from the "stump of Jesse" (the people who would be left after Judah's captivity and return). *Read Isaiah 11:1-9.*

1. Which of these verses do you think refer to
  - Old Testament times
  - New Testament times
  - times yet to come

2. What does Isaiah say Jesus will be like?

3. What characteristic (vv. 2-5) is important for you today to help you trust him more, so he may "dwell [more fully] in your hearts through faith" (Ephesians 3:17)?

4. How does Jesus relate to people in this passage, especially verses 3-4?

5. What could you learn about the Trinity in this passage—God the Father, Jesus the Son, and the Holy Spirit (vv. 2-3)?

6. How do the various aspects of the Spirit (mentioned in v. 2 and listed below) equip Jesus to be the righteous and faithful doer of justice described in verses 3-5?

- Spirit of wisdom and understanding?
- Spirit of counsel and of might?
- knowledge and fear of the Lord?

7. What image (or picture) in this passage is most powerful to you and why?

- a new, small twig blossoms out of a nearly extinct stump (the remnant of Judah that existed in New Testament times) (v. 1)
- words so powerful they act as weapons (v. 4)
- a person so good and devoted that these qualities are fixed in him the way a belt and sash hold clothes on snugly (v. 5)
- a wolf and a lamb (two natural, habitual foes) are perfectly reconciled (v. 6)
- a baby is able to play safely with snakes that are deadly on earth (v. 8)
- another image you find in the passage

8. Why do you think verses 6-9 are often subtitled "paradise regained"?

9. How do you need to study Scripture in a more fruitful way?

10. What truth(s) in this passage do you need or want to absorb more deeply?

 Forming that truth into a prayer. For example, ask God to help you be a part of an effort that brings enemies together, perhaps intentionally or just by being the kind of person who naturally "promotes peace" (Luke 10:6).

NOW OR LATER

Experiment with one or more of the following.

- Before listening to a sermon or beginning a Bible study, ask God to give you openness and humility to see how it might contradict what you already believe and what needs to be corrected in your life.
- Choose a Scripture passage (Sermon on the Mount; 1 John; Psalms 145–150) and read it every day for a month. Pay attention to what you learn each day by jotting down a sentence or two about what you noticed each time.
- Examine Matthew 23:23-29 and John 5:39 to find out how the Pharisees and the teachers of the law managed to study the Scripture so well but miss out on what God was saying.
- Find (in an art book or online site) the painting *The Peaceable Kingdom* by Edward Hicks, a Pennsylvania Quaker (1780–1849). Behind the Isaiah 11 scene, the background features William Penn and a group of Native Americans making treaties. Ponder this painting for a while, and ask God to show you who a modern-day Edward Hicks would paint alongside you. Who do you need to reconcile with?

FOUR

MEDITATION AND OBEDIENCE

Psalm 119:97-104

Y**ou've probably heard** someone say that the longest distance in the world is from a person's head to their heart. What that statement usually means is that to know a fact in your mind does not mean you truly believe it in such a way that your behavior changes. The premise behind this Bible study series is that our behavior changes as we connect with God. When we do the connecting, God does the perfecting.

One of the ways we connect with God is through Scripture, but merely reading Scripture or even studying it is not enough. The connection is extended and made stronger as we meditate on Scripture.

The overlooked discipline of meditation on Scripture is mentioned many times in the Bible—fifteen times in Psalms alone. When Scripture talks about meditation, it often mentions obedience in the next breath: "Keep this Book of the Law always on your lips; *meditate on it day and night, so that you may be careful to do everything written in it.* Then you will be prosperous and successful" (Joshua 1:8, emphasis added). The one who meditates becomes one who obeys (being careful to do).

Group Discussion. If God were to wave a magic wand over you and cause a certain positive character quality to appear (in place of a fault such as grouchiness, laziness, or procrastination), what would you like for the character quality to be?

Personal Reflection. Can you look back at ways God has already changed your inner self?

Psalm 119 connects meditation and obedience. Words such as *meditate, delight,* and *heart* (seeking God with all my heart or setting my heart on God's ways) occur often, as do the words *statute, law, decree,* and *obey.* God does the perfecting as we meditate on Scripture and then let it resonate in our lives all day long. *Read Psalm 119:97-104.*

1. How does the psalmist feel about the law?

2. What does the psalmist do in relation to the law?

3. How is loving the law different from studying the law?

How are they related?

4. If you were to meditate on God's ideas throughout the activities of your day, what activities would lend themselves to ongoing rumination?

5. According to the psalmist, what advantages does meditating on the law bring?

6. The phrases "you yourself have taught me" and "how sweet are your words to my taste" (vv. 102-3) indicate the psalmist's personal connectedness with God through the reading of the recorded words. What, if any, methods of Bible study or meditation create that for you?

7. Even though the psalmist writes a lot about obedience, it isn't expressed with a cold-hearted, teeth-gritting sense of obligation but with great longing for God. How do you explain this?

8. Which style(s) of meditation fit(s) best with the way you process life?

- soaking in and absorbing the meanings of words
- looking for a word or phrase that speaks to you
- picturing the ideas expressed or scenes described in the passage
- enjoying how words are combined (such as obedience and meditation) and connecting the dots between these ideas
- personalizing words of Scripture with specifics by inserting your own everyday activities ("all day long") or common sins ("every evil path") into the text
- reading the passage aloud and waiting for a word or phrase to resonate
- reading it aloud and simply resting or waiting

9. If you were to meditate on a passage and then pray it back to God during a time of prayer or even a mundane activity, what passage of Scripture would that be?

10. As an individual or the leader rereads Psalm 119:97-104 aloud slowly, close your eyes. Notice which phrase stands out to you. Have each group member say aloud the phrase that stands out to them.

Turn your phrase from number 10 into a prayer. For example: O God, help me to savor your thoughts like honey so that they turn into action in my life (v. 103, 101).

NOW OR LATER

Experiment with one or more of the following.

1. Copy Psalm 119:97-104 (or all of Psalm 119) from an electronic concordance and color-code it according to the following themes. Or use symbols for each theme. You may want to do this on your computer if you can copy the text into a file first.

   - *heart* (seeking God with all, setting the heart) = blue or heart shape

   - *law, statutes, decrees, commands, obeying* = red or circle

   - *meditating, delighting* = green or triangle

   Notice how the themes interrelate, especially how the psalmist doesn't just "learn" decrees and statutes but delights in them and meditates on them (vv. 16, 23).

2. Take a walk, bringing along either a Bible or a printed out portion of Scripture. As you walk, put yourself completely into the text and picture yourself as part of it. For example, put yourself into a Gospel story. Imagine yourself as the woman with chronic bleeding who longs for a secret healing (Mark 5:25-34; add vv. 21-24 for greater drama) or the father who only half believes that Jesus can help his demon-possessed son, but sees Jesus heal the boy anyway (Mark 9:14-27).

FIVE

A BIBLICAL MODEL

Luke 1:46-55; 1 Samuel 2:1-10

O ne classic method of entering into a Scripture text is called lectio divina, which is Latin for *divine reading*. Pronounced "lex'-eeoh di-vee'-nuh," it includes reading a Scripture passage aloud, meditating on it, praying about it, and contemplating God in it. As the Bible passage is read, we wait for a word to resonate or "shimmer." Then we meditate on that word or phrase to hear what God might have to say to us. After praying about what this means, we rest in quiet contemplation before God.

The key in lectio is to be open to hear God afresh in Scripture. That means setting aside previous ideas of how this passage applies to us. With unfamiliar passages, it may help to do a short preliminary study to understand historical background and individual words so we can open ourselves to hear anew from God. If we are truly open, God usually communicates surprising things we could never have made up ourselves.

Group Discussion. (To anyone who likes to sing in the car, in the shower, or anywhere that the words aren't printed) How do you feel when you improvise the words of a song because you can't quite remember them?

Personal Reflection. Why do you think singing Scripture is especially meaningful (or why would you, if you don't know any Scripture songs)? What would putting Scripture to music add?

Hannah, a previously infertile woman, asked God for a son and later gave birth to Samuel, which caused her to exalt the Lord (1 Samuel 2). Mary might have been an illiterate peasant girl who lived in a small village. Similar to Hannah, Mary sang a song (Luke 1) when she was pregnant with Jesus. She had gone to visit her cousin Elizabeth, and after Elizabeth called her "mother of my Lord" (v. 43), Mary responded with this song. *Read Luke 1:46-55.*

1. Which phrases, if any, seem particularly lofty or mature for a small-town teenage Jewish girl to be singing?

2. Read 1 Samuel 2:1-10. What themes in this passage are similar to the themes in Luke 1:46-55?

3. In what do both women rejoice?

4. As each woman glorifies God in her song, what qualities of God does each woman mention?

5. People have joked that Mary must have had her Old Testament open to Hannah's song when she sang. How do you explain the similarities?

6. How are the two songs different?

7. How was it possible that Mary could use Hannah's song when Mary had not endured similar circumstances (infertility)?

8. Reread Luke 1:47-55 aloud. Which word or phrase emerges from the passage and stays with you?

9. What is it about that word or phrase that draws you?

10. What might God be inviting you to consider or think about or understand through this word or phrase?

 Pray silently and ask God what he might be calling you to do or refrain from doing through your being drawn to this word or phrase. Then wait quietly, enjoying God's presence.

NOW OR LATER

Experiment with one or more of the following.

- In a private place, sing a song you know by heart (as Mary probably knew Hannah's song). Sing it several times, and let the words of the song deepen within you. If you know American Sign Language, sign the words as you sing.

- Pick a scriptural phrase you have studied in the past. Rest in it, wait in it, and delight in it (but don't analyze it) as you do a physical activity such as mowing the lawn or vacuuming a room.

- Read Genesis 1 and Psalm 8. Compare the ideas and specific words. (Some think Psalm 8 was written as a result of meditating on Genesis 1.) Try meditating on Genesis 1 and writing your own psalm of meditation.

- Pick a passage of Scripture that speaks to you but is not so familiar that it cannot be fresh. Read it aloud to yourself and answer questions 8-10 above.

SIX

ENTERING A GOSPEL SCENE

Mark 10:17-23

A nother common method of meditating on Scripture is to use the imagination and enter the biblical scene as an observer— a fly on the wall or a bystander in the crowd. This common method is what the Israelites did when they celebrated Passover. They rehearsed the historical event from their exodus as slaves in Egypt. To recreate the event, they wore traveling clothes and ate special foods. Likewise, we can recreate a scene from Scripture, asking ourselves what we would see, hear, smell, touch, or taste if we had been present in the biblical scene. As we hear the dialogue of the text, we need to let God speak to us, ask us questions, challenge us, or comfort us.

This imagination-oriented method is *word* centered. The exact words of Scripture coach your imagination. Like lectio divina, certain words or phrases stand out, but in this method we imagine hearing these words said or saying them ourselves.

Are you reluctant to use your imagination for spiritual growth? C. S. Lewis said that reading George MacDonald's fantasies "converted" or "baptized" his imagination. Let meditating on Scripture baptize yours.

Group Discussion. What does a person have to be like to confront another in a genuine but loving way?

Personal Reflection. When, if ever, has someone confronted you in a loving, genuine way? How did that feel to you?

In several places in the Gospels, the authors emphasize how Jesus looked at people (for example, Mark 3:5, 34; 5:32; 8:25, 33; Luke 22:61). Often readers assume certain attitudes go with his look, but it works best to look at the context to see what that look may have entailed. This passage tells us plainly what Jesus' look involved (v. 21), so we don't have to guess. Let's look at this very personal interaction between Jesus and a knowledgeable and earnest young man who also happened to be rich. *Read Mark 10:17-23.*

1. How would you describe the manner of the rich young ruler as he approached Jesus?

2. What do you make of Jesus' answer about what a person must do to inherit eternal life?

Based on Jesus' behavior and words, what seems to have been in his heart when he replied to the young man (v. 21)?

3. What spiritual crisis seems to have occurred within this young man (v. 22)?

4. Reread Mark 10:17-23 (aloud). If you put yourself in the place of the young man as he approaches Jesus, how do you feel as you ask the initial question about inheriting eternal life (v. 17)?

5. Try to picture the moment when Jesus answers the young man. What expression do you see on Jesus' face based on the words of Scripture?

What tone of voice would have matched that facial expression?

6. Imagine that you're the young man. What does it feel like to be invited to be a follower of this great teacher Jesus, but unable to make the choice that will allow you to do so?

7. What is the most stunning thing to you about this passage? Why?

- Jesus invited the young man to be a follower.
- Jesus' ability to be unyieldingly firm, but with great love.
- Jesus' unwillingness to minimize or strike a deal—his insistence that discipleship involves complete reliance on God.
- Something else?

8. What might God be saying to you today through this passage?

- Give up this thing that blocks your reliance on me.
- Take another small step toward giving up this thing I've asked you to give up many times before.
- Hear the love in my voice even as I confront you.
- I still want you as a follower, in spite of . . .
- You won't know the treasure of heaven here on earth until you've . . .
- Look at the people around you—they're more important than the physical things you treasure.
- Something else?

9. How might your relationship with God be affected if you practiced this sort of meditation?

Depending on what came to you out of this text, set aside some time this week to pray—to say directly to God what you need to say about this.

NOW OR LATER

Experiment with one or more of the following.

- Retell your favorite Bible story (to yourself if no one else), but put yourself in the main character's place and tell it as if it were about you.

- Read Luke 13:10-13 and act it out. Take the role of the main character and imagine you've been crippled for eighteen years. You're sitting in the synagogue, completely bent over, listening to the Teacher. Get up and walk bent over at least eighteen steps—one for every year. Walk to the front of the synagogue bent over (the length of a large room) as Jesus calls you forward. Hear Jesus' voice free you from your infirmity. Feel Jesus' hands on you, releasing it. Straighten up and praise God. What do you say? How do you feel?

- Imagine being baptized and journal about it. How could this save you from repeated sins? How could this change your behavior?

---

*C. S. Lewis, introduction to George MacDonald, *Phantastes* (Grand Rapids: Eerdmans, 2000), xi.

LEADER'S NOTES

My grace is sufficient for you.

2 CORINTHIANS 12:9

eading a Bible discussion can be an enjoyable and rewarding experience. But it can also be scary—especially if you've never done it before. If this is your feeling, you're in good company. When God asked Moses to lead the Israelites out of Egypt, he replied, "Please send someone else" (Exodus 4:13)! It was the same with Solomon, Jeremiah, and Timothy, but God helped these people in spite of their weaknesses, and he will help you as well.

You don't need to be an expert on the Bible or a trained teacher to lead a Bible discussion. The idea behind these inductive studies is that the leader guides group members to discover for themselves what the Bible has to say. This method of learning will allow group members to remember much more of what is said than a lecture would.

These studies are designed to be led easily. As a matter of fact, the flow of questions through the passage from observation to interpretation to application is so natural that you may feel that the studies lead themselves. This study guide is also flexible. You can use it with a variety of groups—student, professional, neighborhood, or church groups. Each study takes forty-five to sixty minutes in a group setting.

There are some important facts to know about group dynamics and encouraging discussion. The suggestions listed below should enable you to effectively and enjoyably fulfill your role as leader.

PREPARING FOR THE STUDY

1. Ask God to help you understand and apply the passage in your own life. Unless this happens, you will not be prepared to lead others. Pray too for the various members of the group. Ask God to open your hearts to the message of his Word and motivate you to action.

2. Read the introduction to the guide to get an overview of the entire book and the issues that will be explored.

3. As you begin each study, read and re-read the assigned Bible passage to familiarize yourself with it.

4. This study guide is based on the New International Version of the Bible. It will help you and the group if you use this translation as the basis for your study and discussion.

5. Carefully work through each question in the study. Spend time in meditation and reflection as you consider how to respond.

6. Write your thoughts and responses in the space provided in the study guide. This will help you to express your understanding of the passage clearly.

7. It might help to have a Bible dictionary handy. Use it to look up any unfamiliar words, names, or places. (For additional help on how to study a passage, see chapter five of *How to Lead a LifeBuilder Study*, IVP, 2018.)

8. Consider how you can apply the Scripture to your life. Remember that the group will follow your lead in responding to the studies. They will not go any deeper than you do.

9. Once you have finished your own study of the passage, familiarize yourself with the leader's notes for the study you are leading. These are designed to help you in several ways. First, they tell you the purpose the study guide author had in mind when writing the study. Take time to think through how the study questions work together to accomplish that purpose. Second, the notes provide you with additional background information or suggestions on group dynamics for various questions. This information can be useful when people have difficulty understanding or answering a question. Third, the leader's notes can alert you to potential problems you may encounter during the study.

10. If you wish to remind yourself of anything mentioned in the leader's notes, make a note to yourself below that question in the study.

LEADING THE STUDY

1. Begin the study on time. Open with prayer, asking God to help the group to understand and apply the passage.

2. Be sure that everyone in your group has a study guide. Encourage the group to prepare beforehand for each discussion by reading the introduction to the guide and by working through the questions in the study.

3. At the beginning of your first time together, explain that these studies are meant to be discussions, not lectures. Encourage the members of the group to participate. However, do not put pressure on those who may be hesitant to speak during the first few sessions. You may want to suggest the following guidelines to your group.

- Stick to the topic being discussed.
- Your responses should be based on the verses that are the focus of the discussion and not on outside authorities such as commentaries or speakers.
- These studies focus on a particular passage of Scripture. Only rarely should you refer to other portions of the Bible. This allows for everyone to participate in in-depth study on equal ground.
- Anything said in the group is considered confidential and will not be discussed outside the group unless specific permission is given to do so.
- We will listen attentively to each other and provide time for each person present to talk.
- We will pray for each other.

4. Have a group member read the introduction at the beginning of the discussion.

5. Every session begins with a group discussion question. The question or activity is meant to be used before the passage is read. The question introduces the theme of the study and encourages group members to begin to open up. Encourage as many members as possible to participate, and be ready to get the discussion going with your own response.

This section is designed to reveal where our thoughts or feelings need to be transformed by Scripture. That is why it is especially important not to read the passage before the discussion question is asked. The passage will tend to color the honest reactions people would otherwise give because they are, of course, supposed to think the way the Bible does.

You may want to supplement the group discussion question with an icebreaker to help people get comfortable. See the community section of the *Small Group Starter Kit* (IVP, 1995) for more ideas.

You also might want to use the personal reflection question with your group. Either allow a time of silence for people to respond individually or discuss it together.

6. Have a group member (or members if the passage is long) read aloud the passage to be studied. Then give people several minutes to read the passage again silently so that they can take it all in.

7. Question 1 will generally be an overview question designed to briefly survey the passage. Encourage the group to look at the whole passage, but try to avoid getting sidetracked by questions or issues that will be addressed later in the study.

8. As you ask the questions, keep in mind that they are designed to be used just as they are written. You may simply read them aloud. Or you may prefer to express them in your own words.

There may be times when it is appropriate to deviate from the study guide. For example, a question may have already been answered. If so, move on to the next question. Or someone may raise an important question not covered in the guide. Take time to discuss it, but try to keep the group from going off on tangents.

9. Avoid answering your own questions. If necessary, repeat or rephrase them until they are clearly understood. Or point out something you read in the leader's notes to clarify the context or meaning. An eager group quickly becomes passive and silent if they think the leader will do most of the talking.

10. Don't be afraid of silence. People may need time to think about the question before formulating their answers.

11. Don't be content with just one answer. Ask, "What do the rest of you think?" or "Anything else?" until several people have given answers to the question.

12. Acknowledge all contributions. Try to be affirming whenever possible. Never reject an answer. If it is clearly off base, ask, "Which verse led you to that conclusion?" or again, "What do the rest of you think?"

13. Don't expect every answer to be addressed to you, even though this will probably happen at first. As group members become more at ease, they will begin to truly interact with each other. This is one sign of healthy discussion.

14. Don't be afraid of controversy. It can be very stimulating. If you don't resolve an issue completely, don't be frustrated. Move on and keep it in mind for later. A subsequent study may solve the problem.

15. Periodically summarize what the group has said about the passage. This helps to draw together the various ideas mentioned and gives continuity to the study. But don't preach.

16. At the end of the Bible discussion you may want to allow group members a time of quiet to work on an idea under "Now or Later." Then discuss what you experienced. Or you may want to encourage group members to work on these ideas between meetings. Give an opportunity during the session for people to talk about what they are learning.

17. Conclude your time together with conversational prayer, adapting the prayer suggestion at the end of the study to your group. Ask for God's help in following through on the commitments you've made.

18. End on time.

Many more suggestions and helps are found in *How to Lead a LifeBuilder Study.*

COMPONENTS OF SMALL GROUPS

A healthy small group should do more than study the Bible. There are four components to consider as you structure your time together.

Nurture. Small groups help us to grow in our knowledge and love of God. Bible study is the key to making this happen and is the foundation of your small group.

Community. Small groups are a great place to develop deep friendships with other Christians. Allow time for informal interaction before and after each study. Plan activities and games that will help you get to know each other. Spend time having fun together going on a picnic or cooking dinner together.

Worship and prayer. Your study will be enhanced by spending time praising God together in prayer or song. Pray for each other's needs and keep track of how God is answering prayer in your group. Ask God to help you to apply what you are learning in your study.

Outreach. Reaching out to others can be a practical way of applying what you are learning, and it will keep your group from becoming self-focused. Host a series of evangelistic discussions for your friends or neighbors. Clean up the yard of an elderly friend. Serve at a soup kitchen together, or spend a day working in the community.

Many more suggestions and helps in each of these areas are found in the *Small Group Starter Kit*. You will also find information on building a small group. Reading through the starter kit will be worth your time.

Before each study, you may want to put an asterisk by the key questions you think are most important for your group to cover, in case you don't have time to cover all the questions. As we suggested in "Getting the Most Out of *Study & Meditation*," if you want to make sure you have enough time to discuss all the questions, you have other options. For example, the group could decide to extend each meeting to ninety minutes or more. Alternatively, you could devote two sixty-minute sessions to each study.

STUDY 1. IMMERSING YOURSELF IN GOD'S
THOUGHTS, DEUTERONOMY 6:1-9

PURPOSE: To become thoroughly familiar with Scripture, not just for the sake of knowledge but to connect with God and be coached by God on how to live a life of wholeness.

Question 1. They would fear the Lord and enjoy long life. This helps us see that knowledge of Scripture is not a goal in itself but God's coaching for wise living. *Coaching* is an appropriate word because God comes alongside us in Scripture, offering instruction, models, and encouragement.

Question 2. We struggle to believe that God offers us the best possible life, of a sort of goodness that is appealing. The enemy of our soul convinces us that God is a killjoy, when God is actually the giver of real joy. Sometimes obeying God is difficult, but Scripture helps us connect with God and learn that "the burden is light."

Question 3. Things would go well with them, and their lives would flow with untold benefits in the Promised Land.

Question 4. With a holy, healthy fear of God (v. 2), we look to God as the one who loves us completely and holds the keys to the transformed life. Observing God's commands wipes away the falseness we gravitate toward and leads us to live in wholeness. God's commands teach us how to build genuine relationships with others. They do not lead to a horrible life of depriving ourselves of the goodies we want.

Question 5. God was not like the false Canaanite gods who required capricious acts of worship (such as sacrificing children). Verse 5 makes it clear that the Old Testament is not a collection of rules with no emphasis on relationship with God. Obedience is not found in constantly focusing on self and behavioral failures but in thoroughly immersing oneself in God: heart, soul, and strength.

Says J. A. Thompson, "Obedience was not to spring from a barren legalism based on necessity and duty. It was to arise from a relationship based on love" (J. A. Thompson, *Deuteronomy*, Tyndale Old Testament Commentaries [Downers Grove, IL: InterVarsity Press, 1976], 122).

Question 6. To obey God in a full-hearted way requires a belief that God can be trusted to meet our needs, to care for us, not to do us harm. We need to trust that we're not going to need to lie or to steal to get our needs met. If we truly believe God has what we need and can meet our needs, we're more eager to read Scripture.

Question 7. Talking about God to a child can help adults simplify difficult concepts such as omnipotence and atonement and focus on basic but central truths (God loves you, God wants you to love and obey). This thinking process helps parents as well as children.

Question 8. Constant exposure to God's words creates an ongoing conversation between God and the reader. God becomes "the subject of conversation both inside and outside the home, from the beginning of the day to the end of the day. . . . The commandments were to permeate every sphere of the life of man" (Peter C. Craigie, *The Book of Deuteronomy*, New International Commentary on the Old Testament [Grand Rapids: Eerdmans, 1976], 170). We begin to trust that God speaks to us regularly through the Word.

Question 9. Obedience flows from the central motive and activity—to love God with everything you've got. It involves having the textured heart of a deeply good person.

Question 10. God is transforming our souls, "draw[ing] men into Christ, to make them little Christs," to make people the "same kind of thing as himself" (C. S. Lewis, *Mere Christianity* [New York: Macmillan, 1970], 169, 162).

Question 11. Because they're coming to know God, they are developing a deep-down wisdom and goodness, void of pretension or religiosity.

SESSION 2. READING AND RESPONDING TO SCRIPTURE, NEHEMIAH 8:1-18; 9:1-3, 38

PURPOSE: To respond to Scripture in many ways, including prayer, worship, weeping, celebrating, and confessing sin.

Group Discussion. Keep this lighthearted with your own answers, such as imitating how we fall asleep or try to remember what a favorite radio preacher said.

Read Nehemiah 8:1-9. If reading aloud, you may say the first letter of the names in verses 4 and 7 instead of trying to pronounce them.

Question 1. The Israelites had experienced God as their helper. This made them hungry for more of God and more anxious to discover how to live as God prescribed.

Question 2. This group included men, women, and anyone who could understand—probably older children. They listened attentively.

Question 3. See verse 6. They stood up. They lifted their hands. They bowed their heads and worshiped with faces on the ground. They *responded*—they seem to have been praying.

Question 4. Ezra and the Levites seem to have offered explanations of Scripture, but "making it clear" also included translating it for those who spoke only Aramaic. They set an example of diligence in Scripture reading or "correctly handl[ing] the word of truth" (2 Timothy 2:15).

To help make Scripture clear to ourselves, we may need to examine the background of a passage and compare it with other passages to understand the "whole counsel of God" (Acts 20:27 NKJV). Using a commentary and reading parallel passages are helpful. Noticing the theme of the passage and how each verse relates to that is very important.

This passage will show that studying Scripture is an important preliminary activity, serving the goal of knowing God and interacting with this living God. Then I open the Bible with anticipation that God is going to impart to me today what I need to know.

Question 5. They wept. They experienced what is described in Hebrews 4:12: "For the word of God is alive and active. Sharper than any double-edged sword, it penetrates even to dividing soul and spirit, joints and marrow; it judges the thoughts and attitudes of the heart."

Question 6. To read Scripture without this expectation neglects to let these God-breathed words interrupt our lives so that God can teach us, rebuke us, correct us, and train us (2 Timothy 3:16).

Question 7. Nehemiah urged them to celebrate; this was not mere revelry but a "joy founded on the feeling of the communion with the Lord, on the consciousness that we have in the Lord a God long-suffering and abundant in goodness and truth" (C. F. Keil, *Commentary on the Old Testament*, vol. 3, *I and II Kings, I and II Chronicles, Ezra, Nehemiah, Esther* [Grand Rapids: Eerdmans, 1973], 232). The Levites urged them to "be still" as in Psalm 46:10, "Be still, and know that I am God."

Anytime people understand "the words that had been made known to them" in Scripture (v. 12), a dramatic response, such as this celebration, is appropriate. Scriptural clarity challenges our will, and we need to respond. The consequences of not doing so are described in the old saying "Impression without expression causes depression."

Question 8. These returned exiles built booths and lived in them, celebrating the Feast of Booths, which had not been celebrated since the time of Joshua. This feast was a harvest festival, commemorating the beginning of the forty years of wandering in the wilderness (Exodus 23:16). During the festival, people lived in tents or booths in Jerusalem to remind themselves of how their ancestors lived as they wandered. However, it was a joyous festival, full of games and dancing.

Question 9. They confessed their sins and worshiped God. They made written agreements with each other about how they would behave in the future. It's as if they said, "What I heard leads me to do . . . Help me." In *Praying the Word* Enzo Bianchi advises, "You should make some practical resolutions which are based on your state in life and your position in society, always allowing the Word to be the guiding force in your life" (Enzo Bianchi, *Praying the Word* [Kalamazoo, MI: Cistercian Publications, 1998], 81).

Question 10. Someone might protest that these must be spontaneous and cannot be planned. But they can be deliberate responses to Scripture. Weeping or celebration may not come automatically, but we can journal about reasons the Scripture we read might make us want to weep or celebrate.

Question 11. Back-and-forth conversation with God through Scripture reading builds a relationship that changes a person where simple efforts to obey commands will not.

SESSION 3. COMPREHENDING GOD'S TRUTH, ISAIAH 11:1-9

PURPOSE: To study Scripture to comprehend what the Holy Spirit is communicating through it to give us a better knowledge of God.

Group Discussion. Ask which methods, attitudes, or settings help most. Be open to ideas other than those in the introduction. Because people have different styles of learning, different approaches work, such as analytical methods of Bible study; reading different versions of the Bible; investigating online resources; interacting with others to stimulate thinking; simple, commonsense approaches taken by a particular speaker or a series of studies; coming up with hunches from a passage and following up with other passages to see if those hunches are true; connecting truth in Scripture to truth in art and literature.

Question 1. Verse 1: the stump of Jesse refers to King David of the Old Testament; the shoot and Branch are the Messiah who we know is Jesus. Verses 2-3 may refer to Jesus in the New Testament. Verses 3-9 refer to times yet to come, including Revelation in the New Testament. Verses 3-5 may refer to Jesus' behavior in the Gospels.

It could be said that verses 6-9, about natural enemies being at peace with each other, referred (in certain moments) to New Testament situations such as the apostles' diverse backgrounds working together (Simon the revolutionary zealot and Matthew the government's tax collector) or even some of the political and social diversity in churches such as Philippians (a former slave girl, a government prison guard, and Lydia, a rich woman [Acts 16:11-40]). These verses could also point us toward further off eschatological events.

Isaiah spoke to the Northern Kingdom of Judah in Old Testament times about their upcoming captivity. His message is about the time everlasting—the "peaceable kingdom" of heaven (vv. 6-9).

Question 2. The Spirit of the Lord will rest on Jesus, and he will delight in the fear of the Lord. Jesus will not be fooled by outward appearances but will judge with integrity based on righteousness and faithfulness.

Question 4. (This question begins the second cycle of observe, interpret, and apply questions.) The Lord looks at the heart, not outward appearances (1 Samuel 16:7). In fact, verse 4 says he will judge the poor with righteousness. The poor and the humble—who do not catch a break—will finally get the help and respect they need. (Studying the meaning of words in their original language can help us.)

The odd picture in the last phrase of verse 4 about striking the earth with the "rod of his mouth" is understood better when we remember that prophets such as Isaiah spoke to idolatrous people. They were not listened to, so they often used arresting, even odd, word pictures to get listeners' attention. Isaiah referred to Jesus' words and breath, though not physical entities, as being so strong they would be capable of punishment and death.

Question 5. The Spirit rests on the Son who then delights in but stands in awe of God the Father. You might ask participants if this enlightens or contradicts their current understanding of the Trinity. Honest study requires that we remain open to the Scriptures contradicting what we already know or think. Reconciling seeming contradictions often helps us think more clearly and understand more of God's infinite greatness.

Question 6. Here are some ideas:

What Jesus is like	This equips Jesus to be
Spirit of wisdom and understanding	a guide for his people
Spirit of counsel and power	a guardian for this people
Knowledge and fear of the Lord	an example for his people

Question 8. A place in which natural enemies get along (for example, the wolf living with the lamb) and safe from all danger (for example, an infant playing near a cobra's den) describes not only the Garden of Eden but also "a new heaven and a new earth, where righteousness dwells" (2 Peter 3:13, "dwells" meaning goodness and righteousness are the normal way of doing things.) See also Revelation 21.

Question 9. Here are some possibilities you may suggest:

- God brings redemption and reconciliation (Jesus) out of failure (the remnant of Judah).
- The community of the Trinity: the Spirit interacts with Jesus in the fear of God (v. 2).
- God judges not by outward appearance but with true rightness and justice.
- In the kingdom of God, bitter enemies (including those in the animal world) no longer have fierce conflicts but live together peaceably.

Now or Later. Encourage participants to try one of the exercises. The second exercise is helpful for those who learn better through repetition rather than asking formal questions. The third one is for those who love looking for clues and drawing conclusions. The last exercise may help those who are more visual or imaginative.

SESSION 4. MEDITATION AND OBEDIENCE, PSALM 119:97-104

PURPOSE: To connect with God, which leads to obedience.

Question 1. The psalmist seems quite excited about the law! Notice phrases such as "I love your law" (v. 97) and "How sweet are your words to my taste" (v. 103).

You may wonder what "the law" is that we love and meditate on. The law includes the Ten Commandments, Leviticus, Deuteronomy, and *all* the instructions we find in the Old Testament. But Jesus taught us that all these guidelines can be distilled into two commands: *love God* and *love others* (Matthew 22:36-40). New Testament passages such as the Sermon on the Mount (Matthew 5–7), Colossians 3:1-17, and Romans 12:9-21 explain how to become the kind of person who obeys the law—not placing anything before God, not taking God's name in vain, not murdering people even in our thoughts.

If you think it would be helpful, explain the previous paragraph and ask the participants' permission to substitute a phrase such as "God's ideas" or "God's way of doing things" for *law*.

If someone protests that Christians are not "under the law," explain that Christ's coming, death, and resurrection fulfilled the law but did not abolish it. Although we are justified by grace (not the law), the law describes the deep goodness of God. Paul's words in Romans 7:22, "For in my inner being I delight in God's law," resemble Psalm 119:97. What we want to avoid is trying to be justified or supposedly earning salvation by law keeping or being self-righteous about obeying God's commands (Galatians 5:4; Luke 11:52). If further discussion is required, set aside another time to look at Romans 7:4-12, 8 and Galatians 3, 5.

Question 2. The psalmist meditates on the law, keeps the commands always with him (at the front of the mind), doing what the law says (obeying).

Question 3. Having studied the law and found a treasure, one loves it by thinking about it and giving up everything else to bask in it.

(Consider the parable of the man who found the treasure buried in the field and gave up everything to have it. How he must have pondered it, imagined himself owning it, thought about how wonderful the treasure was, and wondered that he was going to own it himself!) Loving the law is like this. It is worth the time to bask in Scripture and taste and see that the Lord is good.

Question 4. Physical activities, especially walking, running, riding a bike, or gardening are excellent. In fact, you can train yourself to do this by doing these activities after you spend time soaking in the Word and loving it. Sometimes relatively mindless activities work well—running errands, mowing the lawn, and washing dishes.

Question 5. Focusing on God's ways of doing things makes us wiser than the people who oppose us (v. 98), gives us more insight than teachers (v. 99), more understanding than those considered wise (v. 100), helps us do the right thing (vv. 100-102), and understand why (v. 104).

Question 6. You may wish to point out that this psalm is a very personal one. Verses 4-176 all have a personal pronoun you or your in them, referring to God. This underscores the personal admiration and joy in what God says (the law) that comes to those who meditate on it. If few participants have an answer for the kind of Bible reading that helps them, be ready to give an example from your own experience. You might want to mention that someone who loves God's law is convinced that God's principles for goodness are not only to be cherished (v. 103) but also give exceptional wisdom.

Question 7. Meditation is a very relational discipline in which you give yourself—your deeper thoughts, imaginings, and inner brooding—to God. God can use that part of yourself to teach you to long for all who God is.

Question 9. Encourage participants to choose passages they've recently studied and understood, or familiar passages (the Lord's Prayer, Psalm 23) can be excellent.

Question 10. Offer to read the passage aloud at this time and let participants rest in the passage and then write their answers. Allow at least seven to ten minutes.

Prayer suggestion. After participants have said aloud their phrase, invite them to open their eyes. Ask, Would anyone like to tell us what they think God might be saying to them—or inviting them to think about or do—today through this passage?

SESSION 5. A BIBLICAL MODEL, LUKE 1:46-55; 1 SAMUEL 2:1-10

PURPOSE: To learn the lectio divina method, which will help us follow Mary's example.

Group Discussion. While sometimes we're frustrated when we don't know the words, other times we come up with very clever substitutions—especially when we truly love the song!

Question 1. Her soul glorifying the Lord (v. 46), thinking all generations would call her blessed (v. 48), political situations (v. 52).

Question 2. If possible, print out a sheet or create a slide that has the two passages side by side. Otherwise, read 1 Samuel 2:1-10 aloud again and ask participants to continue looking at Luke 1:46-55 and stop you when you hear something similar to the Luke passage. Here are some suggestions: heart, spirit, and soul rejoice in the Lord; God is holy; the proud do not succeed; the hungry are no longer hungry; the Lord raises up the poor; God guards faithful servants.

Question 3. Both rejoice in God. They delight in and celebrate God's own self not simply in benefits received or results hoped for, but because of who he is (1 Samuel 2:1; Luke 1:47).

Question 4. Mary sings that God's name is holy (v. 49). Hannah says no one is holy like God (v. 2). She also says that God is unique and a rock. They are both marveling at God's initiative and God's actions, which demonstrate God's power.

Question 5. Many believe Mary was singing from her heart based on what had been cultivated there through meditating on Hannah's song, perhaps even singing it as a "household song" as she worked at home. (Mary also borrows phrases from several psalms, including Psalm 71:19; 98:1; 98:3; 103:17; 107:9; 111:9; 132:11; 138:6. When improvising on a song we know by heart, we often do the same—borrowing lines from other songs. Noting the similarities between the women's songs, commentator Norval Geldenhuys writes, "All pious Israelites from their childhood days knew by heart songs from the Old Testament and often sang them in the home circle and at celebrations. Mary was steeped in the poetical literature of her nation, and accordingly her hymn also bears the unmistakable signs of it" (Norval Geldenhuys, *The Gospel of Luke*, New International Commentary on the New Testament [Grand Rapids: Eerdmans, 1977], 85).

Question 6. Geldenhuys points out, "While Mary sings her happiness with deep humility and holy reserve, Hannah completely surrenders herself to a feeling of personal triumph over her enemies. Where Mary borrowed expressions from the Old Testament, she gives to the consecrated words a deep meaning and higher application" (Geldenhuys, *Gospel of Luke*, 85).

Question 7. Although Mary's situation was different, she identified with many of the scriptural truths expressed in Hannah's song. When Scripture has been meditated on and "written in the heart," it has personal meaning and can be transferred and personalized to many situations.

Question 8. Before reading the passage aloud, ask participants to close their eyes. Invite them to come to the text with an open mind and heart to receive. To benefit especially the men in the group, preface the reading by saying something about how this passage can be a song for women and men who have felt that God would have no reason to choose to use them in any special way.

Then have the passage read aloud slowly, with equal weight given to each word. Urge participants to wait quietly in the silence afterward to see what word stands out or resonates, creating sort of a "'holding pattern' on just one sentence (or one word)" (Robert Mulholland, *Shaped by the Word* [Nashville: Upper Room, 2000], 55).

After a few minutes, ask them to share that word with the group.

SESSION 6. ENTERING A GOSPEL SCENE, MARK 10:17-23

PURPOSE: To learn Ignatian meditation, using the imagination.

Group Discussion. When we're confronted, it's often in a mean-spirited tone. But a loving confrontation can have a transforming effect on us because we can see the person loves us—meaning they want what is best for us and can be kind about it.

Question 1. He ran up to meet Jesus with enthusiasm even though Jesus was "on his way." He fell before him, which would indicate one of two things. Either he truly adored Jesus from watching him and hearing him, or he was being obsequious and fawning, making a big fuss over Jesus. Commentator Will Lane chooses the former:

> The eager approach of a man while Jesus was setting out on his way, his kneeling posture, the formal address together with the weighty character of his question—all suggest deep respect for Jesus and genuine earnestness on the part of the man himself. (William Lane, *The Gospel According to Mark*, New International Commentary on the New Testament [Grand Rapids: Eerdmans, 1975], 364)

Parallel passages tell us the man was young (Matthew 19:20) and a ruler (Luke 18:18).

Question 2. Jesus was not at odds with the law. He saw in the Old Testament law the key components of discipleship. Jesus seems to be drawing the man forward by appealing to the law, which the young man would have been quite familiar with. Jesus was putting his finger on the man's hunger.

If someone comments on Jesus' refusal to accept the descriptor "good," you might reply with this clarification by Will Lane: "In

the Old Testament and subsequent Judaism only God is charac-
teristically called 'good,' although it was possible to speak in a
derived sense of 'the good man' (Prov. 12:2; 14:14, others)" (Lane,
Gospel According to Mark, 364).

Question 3. Jesus' look of love communicates that he had a tender
heart of love and that he was skilled at speaking the truth in love
(Ephesians 4:15). Jesus also must have had a high opinion of the
young man since he invited him to become a follower! Still, Jesus
was tough, insisting the young man would have to do what the
Twelve had done—abandon everything to follow him.

Question 4. Initially so eager to please Jesus, the rich young man
gave up the invitation to become a follower of Jesus because he
couldn't let go of something he loved more. No wonder his face fell.
Says Hugh Anderson: "Since this man is captive to what the world
has offered him he is not free to receive God's offer [of discipleship],
vexed though he is to say No to it" (Hugh Anderson, *The Gospel of
Mark*, New Century Bible Commentary [Grand Rapids: Eerdmans,
1981], 250).

Question 5. Before reading the passage aloud (even if you're doing
the study by yourself), explain that the previous four questions
helped the group study the basic words and ideas of the text. Now
it's time to read the text again and *enter into it*.

If you wish, ask participants to close their eyes and imagine themselves as this young man before they answer. He seems to have been
very confident: "The inquirer's idea of goodness was defined by
human achievement. He regarded himself as 'good' in that he had
fulfilled the commandments. . . . Now he hopes to discover from another 'good' man what he can do to assure eternal life" (Lane, *Gospel
According to Mark*, 365).

If you have time after answering this question, ask participants
to put themselves in the place of some disciples standing by. Are
they embarrassed by this man's kneeling or his bold interruption?

Question 6. Participants will need to close their eyes to picture an expression on Jesus' face based on the words of the text. The words *loved him* "may denote either that [Jesus] openly showed affection by putting his arms around him or had the profoundest sympathy for his need" (Anderson, *Gospel of Mark*, 249). A certain earnestness in Jesus is appropriate too, given that he invites the young man to be one of his followers.

Question 7. Suggest that participants try letting their own faces move from expressions of eagerness to disappointment to see how that facial movement affects them inside. It must have been an episode of roller-coaster emotions: first the youth's intense enthusiasm and devotion, then his disappointment.

Question 9. Ask participants to close their eyes. Explain that you're going to read the passage aloud to them once more, then ask the question. Urge them not to jump at an easy answer or feel as if they have to make something up. When we sit quietly before God, God often has surprising things to say to us. They may want to ask themselves: *What question is God asking me through this text?*

After you've asked the question and waited a few minutes, ask participants who are willing to say what came to them. If nothing came to them, that's fine. The quiet provided them a moment to simply enjoy the presence of God.

Jan Johnson is the author of twenty-three books and many Bible studies and lectio divina exercises, including Prayer and Listening *and* Reflection and Confession. *She teaches at several US universities and on the Apprentice Experience, a US discipleship course. For more on Jan, visit www.janjohnson.org.*